REBEL GIRLS

POWERFUL PAIRS

25 TALES OF MOTHERS AND DAUGHTERS

Good Night Stories for Rebel Girls and Rebel Girls are registered trademarks. *Good Night Stories for Rebel Girls* and all other Rebel Girls titles are available for bulk purchase for sale promotions, premiums, fundraising, and educational needs. For details, write to sales@rebelgirls.com.

This is a work of creative nonfiction. It is a collection of heartwarming and thought-provoking stories inspired by the lives and adventures of 51 influential women. It is not an encyclopedic account of the events and accomplishments of their lives.

www.rebelgirls.com

Text by Abby Sher, Jestine Ware, Nana Brew-Hammond, Sam Guss, Sarah Parvis, and Susanna Daniel
Art direction by Giulia Flamini
Cover illustrations by Annalisa Ventura
Graphic design by Annalisa Ventura and Kristen Brittain

Printed in Italy, October 2021
10 9 8 7 6 5 4 3 2 1

ISBN: 978-1-73487-707-6

CONTENTS

INTRODUCTION

Dear Rebels,

Welcome to *Powerful Pairs*, a book about incredible mothers and daughters who embody the Rebel spirit together. A mother-daughter relationship can be so many things— intense, inspiring, supportive, and yes, sometimes frustrating. After all, our mothers are the ones who welcome us into this world and hear our first cries. Whatever happens after that is a true adventure!

In these pages, you will read about well-known pairs, like Beyoncé and her daughter Blue Ivy, and Julie Andrews and her daughter Emma Walton Hamilton. And you will be introduced to new duos, like pilots Laurie and Arianna Strand and rowers Sarah and Sally Kettle. The stories in this book will take you to the fight for women's suffrage in England and to the search for an Alzheimer's vaccine in China.

You will meet women who work together, dance together, and go on amazing, life-changing journeys together. So, grab a hard hat and a hammer and rehab homes with Karen E. Laine and Mina Starsiak Hawk. Kick off your shoes and practice traditional Indian dance moves with Niveditha Shetty Hegde and Ishanvi Hegde. Then pack your bags and hike the Appalachian Trail with Briana and Cambyr Sullivan.

The mothers and daughters in this book challenge and motivate each other. They dare and encourage each other. They share a special bond. And because of this bond, they're able to do extraordinary things, like distribute vaccines and create breathtaking art. They help their communities and explore uncharted waters. They grow and learn together, sharing their gifts with the world.

We hope these tales inspire you and make you smile. Most of all, we want to honor the fact that mother-daughter relationships come in all flavors, shapes, and sizes. We hope what you find in here is a connection to Rebels from the past, the present, and the future. Everyone in this book is like you in some way—full of creativity, determination, and possibility. Always remember that there are people loving and supporting you on your journey and that the Rebel Girls community is growing stronger every day because of you.

Stay Rebel!

SCAN TO HEAR MORE!

BONUS! AUDIO STORIES!
Download the Rebel Girls app to hear longer stories about some of the unstoppable mother-daughter duos in this book. You will also unlock creative activities and discover stories of other trailblazing women. Whenever you come across a bookmark icon, just scan the code, and you'll be whisked away on an audio adventure.

From
REBEL GIRLS

BEYONCÉ AND BLUE IVY CARTER

SINGERS

Once upon a time, there was a girl named Beyoncé who tried to shrink herself. She kept her gaze to the ground, never raised her hand in class, and barely spoke. Why? Because mean girls at school didn't like her light-brown skin.

One day, Beyoncé's first grade teacher taught the class a song. When Beyoncé's mom asked her to sing it, a rush—almost like electricity—charged through Beyoncé's body. Performing while her mother washed the dishes, she had no clue that her electrifying voice would inspire millions of future fans.

To build her confidence, Beyoncé started a singing group, and after some painful rejections, the girls' careers exploded. They sold 60 million records together, and as a solo artist, Beyoncé has sold almost double that!

Still, she's never forgotten who she was when she first sang in her mother's kitchen. When she became a mom, Beyoncé wanted her daughter, Blue Ivy, to know she never had to make herself small so others could feel big.

When Blue was old enough to express her opinion, Beyoncé started asking what she thought about her work. To Beyoncé's relief, Blue said she's always proud of her mom—except when she tells corny jokes.

By eight years old, Blue was singing on Beyoncé's hit "Brown Skin Girl." The song celebrates the power of girls who often get overlooked or bullied for their skin color. It earned Blue her first Grammy. Blue can also be spotted twirling midair in an acrobat's hoop in her mom's latest visual album.

Whatever the future holds for this talented duo, Beyoncé's sure to be right there cheering Blue on and making sure she shrinks for no one.

BEYONCÉ, BORN SEPTEMBER 4, 1981
BLUE IVY, BORN JANUARY 7, 2012
UNITED STATES OF AMERICA

"MOTHERHOOD HAS BEEN MY BIGGEST INSPIRATION. IT BECAME MY MISSION TO MAKE SURE [MY DAUGHTER] LIVED IN A WORLD WHERE SHE FEELS TRULY SEEN AND VALUED."
—BEYONCÉ

ILLUSTRATION BY LAYLIE FRAZIER

SCAN TO HEAR MORE!

BRIANA SULLIVAN AND CAMBYR SULLIVAN

HIKERS

One day, Briana decided she wanted to go on a hike all by herself. Her kids were at summer camp, so it seemed like the perfect time. She left technology behind and headed for the majestic White Mountains. She spent two weeks in nature and loved it—even when it rained! She vowed one day she would hike the whole Appalachian Trail.

Her daughter Cambyr wasn't interested when her mom asked if she wanted to hike. She didn't even like camping that much. But then Cambyr found a video about a whole family that hiked the trail.

So cool! she decided. *Let's do it!*

After talking with Cambyr's teachers, Briana prepared to homeschool her daughter. Cambyr would finish up the eighth grade while walking 10 to 30 miles a day. As they hiked up mountains, explored forests, and crossed rivers, they scavenged for mushrooms, berries, and medicinal plants. They made friends with hikers from all over the world. And every night, Briana played her guitar before they went to sleep.

The pair even picked up hiking names while out on the trail. Briana's new name was Chickweed after the weed she foraged and stuffed into her sandwiches to help soothe the aches and pains from their trek. Cambyr's was Kaleidoscope because her personality is all the colors of the rainbow.

The trail ended at Mount Katahdin in Maine—more than 2,000 miles from where they'd started. Briana stood on the trail sign and raised her guitar above her head in victory while Cambyr snapped a picture. Exhausted and overjoyed, they shouted "Yahoo!" into the sky.

BRIANA, BORN NOVEMBER 21, 1972
CAMBYR, BORN MAY 5, 2006
UNITED STATES OF AMERICA

"FOLLOW ME AND MY AMAZING 13-YEAR-OLD DAUGHTER AS WE PACK OUR BAGS OF DREAMS AND TAKE ONLY AN OUNCE OR TWO OF PRACTICALITY WITH US ON A SIX-MONTH ADVENTURE OF A LIFETIME."
— BRIANA SULLIVAN

ILLUSTRATION BY DEANDRA HODGE

CHANG YI WANG AND MEI MEI HU

BIOTECH FOUNDER AND CEO

Once upon a time, there was a girl who was fascinated by viruses. They were just so tiny and strange! But they can make people very sick. So Chang Yi set out to find ways to outsmart them.

She became a top-notch scientist and started her own company, but her daughter, Mei Mei, wasn't interested in biotechnology. Instead of following in her mom's footsteps to become a scientist, she studied economics and law. While Chang Yi worked hard in her lab, Mei Mei used her skills to help businesses that were in trouble.

One day, Chang Yi invited Mei Mei over for dinner. They got to talking and Mei Mei realized that, this time, it was her mom's company that was in trouble. She couldn't just sit by and do nothing! She knew she had to help.

Mei Mei sifted through her mom's paperwork and made piles. Then she moved to the whiteboard to scribble out a plan. She circled the biggest and best science project Chang Yi was working on: an Alzheimer's vaccine.

Many people all over the world suffer from this disease. It steals people's memories. It can make people get extra cranky, repeat words, forget where they put things or where they are, and even forget to eat and drink.

Mei Mei reorganized the company and started a new venture with her mother. In her lab, Chang Yi cooked up a vaccine that would encourage the brain to attack the nasty plaque that causes Alzheimer's. She'll keep working until it is ready for people.

Mei Mei helped save the company so that Chang Yi could help save people in the future with her life-changing vaccine. They are a mighty team!

CHANG YI, BIRTHDATE UNKNOWN
MEI MEI, BIRTHDATE UNKNOWN
CHINA AND THE UNITED STATES OF AMERICA

"MY PARENTS GAVE ME THE NAME CHANG YI WHICH, IN ENGLISH, MEANS 'ALWAYS HAPPY.' IF WE CURED ALZHEIMER'S, I WOULD BE VERY HAPPY."
—CHANG YI WANG

ILLUSTRATION BY NAN CAO

EMMELINE PANKHURST, CHRISTABEL PANKHURST, AND SYLVIA PANKHURST

SUFFRAGISTS

A long time ago, back when women couldn't own property or vote in elections, Emmeline was born in a village in England. Her teachers were different from others at the time. They didn't care if she was a girl or a boy. They just wanted her to learn.

When she grew up, Emmeline decided to help women by joining some local groups. The groups talked politely about change—but they didn't do anything, which frustrated Emmeline. *What good does it do to just talk?* she wondered. So she created her own group, and she called it the Women's Social and Political Union, or WSPU.

The WSPU did a lot more than talk. They fought for a woman's right to vote. They were not polite or "ladylike" at all. In fact, they were what you'd call *radical*—they started fires and smashed windows and went on hunger strikes. They'd do anything to get the attention of politicians and the press. Emmeline defended her tactics by saying, "We are here, not because we are law-breakers; we are here in our efforts to become law-makers."

Soon, Emmeline's daughters Christabel and Sylvia were old enough to fight for change alongside their mother. Christabel, the oldest of five, earned a law degree but wasn't allowed to practice law because she was a woman. Sylvia, the second oldest, was particularly interested in poverty and working conditions for women. Together, the three activists landed in jail many times. Like any family, they had disagreements. But ultimately, the Pankhursts' efforts paid off and, in 1928, English women were granted the right to vote.

EMMELINE, JULY 14, 1858–JUNE 14, 1928
CHRISTABEL, SEPTEMBER 22, 1880–FEBRUARY 13, 1958
SYLVIA, MAY 5, 1882–SEPTEMBER 27, 1960

UNITED KINGDOM

ILLUSTRATION BY
TATSIANA BURGAUD

VOTES FOR WOMEN

"WE FOUND THAT ALL THE FINE PHRASES ABOUT FREEDOM AND LIBERTY WERE ENTIRELY FOR MALE CONSUMPTION, AND THAT THEY DID NOT IN ANY WAY APPLY TO WOMEN."
—EMMELINE PANKHURST

FARTUUN ADAN AND ILWAD ELMAN

HUMANITARIANS

Once upon a time, there was a war in Somalia. It lasted for decades. As the danger mounted, Fartuun had to make a decision. Would she flee to Canada or stay and try to keep her family safe?

She chose to take her three daughters and run. Her husband, a peace activist, stayed behind and was killed. Fartuun and her girls felt their world crumbling. Their grief was bigger than an ocean. And still, they heard bad news coming from their home country. Bombs went off every day. Children were being recruited as soldiers or kidnapped as child brides.

After many years in Canada, Fartuun decided to do an impossible thing. She would return to Somalia to help as many people as she could.

"Mama, don't go!" her daughters pleaded.

Fartuun thought of all the people who were suffering. "If we just sit somewhere and say, 'I'm safe,' I don't think that's right," she said.

A few years later, when Fartuun's daughter Ilwad was 19, she insisted on joining her mother in Somalia. Fartuun begged her to stay where it was safe. But Ilwad said no. She needed to see her mother in action.

Ilwad and Fartuun worked with their organization, Elman Peace. They saved women and girls from being hurt or kidnapped. They rescued child soldiers and provided them with an education and a place to heal.

Not everybody was happy about their work. Some politicians discouraged them. Some people harassed their staff. Once, they even got shut down! But these two brave women kept their organization going. And they won't stop until all girls have access to education and Somalia is peaceful and safe again.

FARTUUN, BORN FEBRUARY 2, 1969
ILWAD, BORN DECEMBER 22, 1989

SOMALIA AND CANADA

"I SAW MY MOM TRYING SO HARD TO CREATE SAFE SPACES FOR WOMEN AND CHILDREN. I FELL IN LOVE WITH THE WORK AND FOUND MY MISSION."
—ILWAD ELMAN

ILLUSTRATION BY LAYLIE FRAZIER

JEN LEE REEVES AND JORDAN REEVES

DISABILITY ADVOCATES

Jen always said that her daughter Jordan was "born just right." Jordan was born with a limb difference—her left arm ended just above the elbow. Having a disability didn't make Jordan any less "right" than any other kid. She was just doing things her own way.

But there were a few things about having a limb difference that Jordan found frustrating. All these things had to do with other people. Whenever Jordan met someone new, she would slide her left arm behind her back and wonder how the person would react when they saw her arm. Would they stare? Get scared? Say something unkind?

One day, Jordan was in a workshop with other kids like her. They talked about prosthetics, or artificial body parts. The question of the day was: "If you could build anything instead of an arm, what would you make?"

Why do I need to have a hand on the end of my arm, she wondered, *when I could have something way cooler, like . . . a unicorn horn that shoots glitter!*

Jordan worked with an adult on "Project Unicorn." The finished prosthetic was shiny and purple. It showered the world with joy and sparkles! Jordan started thinking, *What if other kids could see their disabilities not as limitations, but as opportunities for creativity and innovation?*

Jen knew her daughter was on to something. So the pair teamed up and started the nonprofit Design With Us to teach kids with disabilities about design and STEAM (science, technology, engineering, art, and mathematics). They want to help others think about products they wish existed and come up with designs that do *exactly* what they want them to do.

JEN, BORN MAY 12, 1974
JORDAN, BORN DECEMBER 29, 2005
UNITED STATES OF AMERICA

ILLUSTRATION BY
BÁRBARA TAMILIN

"AT THE HEART OF IT ALL,
WE ARE TEACHING HOW
TO DESIGN *WITH* OTHERS,
NOT *FOR* OTHERS."
—JEN LEE REEVES

JULIE ANDREWS AND EMMA WALTON HAMILTON

AUTHORS

Emma was just a little girl when she saw a life-size cardboard cutout of Mary Poppins and shouted, *Look! There's Mummy!* Strangers passing by said, *Isn't that sweet? That little girl thinks her mother is Mary Poppins.* They had no idea she was telling the truth!

Emma's mom, Julie Andrews, starred in classic movies like *Mary Poppins* and *The Sound of Music.* Her bright eyes and extraordinary singing voice captivated audiences around the world. But no matter how famous she became in theater and film, her favorite role was always Mom.

Emma was four when her parents got divorced. They wouldn't be together all the time, so Julie and Emma came up with a project for the whole family. When Emma stayed with her mom, they wrote a story. When she visited her dad, he added pictures. That is how they weaved the tale of *Simeon's Gift.*

Julie kept performing all around the world and, as Emma grew up, she started acting too. They even produced a show together called *Julie's Greenroom,* where Julie taught children about performing arts. But when the lights and cameras went off, they both loved to write.

The creative pair started writing children's books together again—and it was a joy! First they published *Dumpy the Dump Truck,* a story about a little boy and his grandfather saving an old truck from the junkyard and going on marvelous adventures. Later, they started a podcast, where listeners can hear them chat, tell stories, and read books aloud in their clear, friendly voices.

Julie and Emma have written more than 30 books for all ages. They share ideas, finish each other's sentences, and absolutely adore working together.

JULIE, BORN OCTOBER 1, 1935
EMMA, BORN NOVEMBER 27, 1962
UNITED KINGDOM

"WHEN WE DO WORK TOGETHER, THE BEST IDEA WINS."
—JULIE ANDREWS

ILLUSTRATION BY
JENNIFER M. POTTER

KAREN E. LAINE AND MINA STARSIAK HAWK

HOME REHABBERS

Once there lived a mother and daughter who wanted everyone to know about their special hometown: Indianapolis. The mom, Karen, worked as a lawyer. But she had other interests too. She had an enormous tattoo on her back and loved to recycle old fixtures and souvenirs. When her daughter, Mina, bought a fixer-upper, Karen said, "We can make this house beautiful." And together, they did.

Starting out, Karen and Mina barely knew a wrench from a screwdriver. They watched videos and asked questions, and soon they knew how to lay tile, hang drywall, make furniture, and wire electricity—all on a tight budget.

In 2008, the pair formed a business called Two Chicks and a Hammer. Working together all day every day was a challenge. They both agreed that Mina acted more like the mom and that Karen was more like the kid. But even when they clashed, their love and trust won out.

Cleaning out dirty, abandoned homes was the hardest part of their work. There was always a lot of animal poop to get rid of! And once, they found a freezer filled with slabs of rotting meat. *Eww!* Demolition, on the other hand, came easily. "No one has to teach you how to break stuff," said Karen.

In 2014, they started hosting their own TV show, *Good Bones*, so they could employ more locals and spotlight small businesses. Mina and Karen helped bring the historic Indianapolis neighborhoods they treasured back to life, one house at a time.

Karen has advice for girls who aspire to repair houses: "You've got to be real, not afraid. You've got to get your hands dirty, along with everyone else."

KAREN, BIRTHDATE UNKNOWN
MINA, BORN NOVEMBER 26, 1987
UNITED STATES OF AMERICA

"THAT'S THE VALUE OF BEING MOTHER AND DAUGHTER—SHE'S NOT GOING TO LOSE ME. I'M ALWAYS GOING TO LOVE HER AND THINK SHE'S AWESOME AND HAVE HER BACK."
—KAREN E. LAINE

ILLUSTRATION BY FANESHA FABRE

KAYUULA NOVALINGA AND SHINA NOVALINGA

THROAT SINGERS

Kayuula and her daughter, Shina, were both born in Nunavik, Canada, which is full of snowcapped mountains, wide sparkling lakes, caribou, and polar bears. Kayuula and Shina are part of the Indigenous Inuit people, who have lived on this land for almost a thousand years. Many Inuits spend time in the wilderness, hunting and harvesting. They are known for their sewing and printmaking, and the way they tell stories through a special kind of music called throat singing.

Standing face to face, Kayuula makes a low, breathy sound. Then, Shina tries to match that sound. Kayuula adds a rhythm with her voice, and Shina does the same. They go back and forth, sometimes with high-pitched bird calls and sometimes with exhales that sound like rushing wind. Pretty soon, it's hard to tell who is leading and who is following.

Throat singing is a sacred tradition for the Inuit. In the early 1900s, colonists who wanted to take over the Inuit lands outlawed throat singing. As time moved on, fewer and fewer people practiced it. But as Shina says, "We are now taking it back and passing it down to keep it alive."

In March 2020, Shina began posting videos of their songs online. People were amazed by their voices. Shina then started sharing insights about Inuit culture and showing off the clothing that Kayuula made for her by hand.

As Shina and Kayuula become more and more popular, they've used their voices not only to sing but also to talk about Indigenous rights and raise money for Indigenous communities in need. They celebrate their past and present and urge people to help protect their future.

KAYUULA, BORN 1977
SHINA, BORN 1998
CANADA

"THE CONNECTION BETWEEN MY MOTHER AND ME GROWS BIGGER AS WE THROAT SING TOGETHER. IT'S ALWAYS A BEAUTIFUL MOMENT FOR US."
—SHINA NOVALINGA

ILLUSTRATION BY
ANDRESSA MEISSNER

KERI SHAHIDI AND YARA SHAHIDI

ACTORS AND PRODUCERS

Yara was a cheerful baby. Photographers and directors wanted to put her in ads and commercials. She started her career when she was just six weeks old! Yara's whole family was in the media business. Her mom, Keri, was a Black American model and actor, and her dad was an Iranian-American photographer. Yara and her two younger brothers enjoyed their modeling and acting gigs.

When Yara was little, her mom told her something she'd never forget: that her ideas and opinions were valuable and worth sharing.

As an actor, Yara followed a script and made characters come to life. But sometimes she thought she'd have more freedom if *she* had more say over the stories being told.

Yara and Keri loved spending time together. Whether they were reading books, jumping rope, or borrowing each other's clothes, they brightened each other's days. When they talked, they asked questions and encouraged one another. Sometimes, their clever ideas tumbled out like the unstoppable rush of a river. They both wanted to tell new stories and work with people who were often left out of the movie-making process. And they wanted to provide more complex and exciting roles for Black writers and actors. So they decided to start a production company together. Soon they were pitching projects and making deals to produce TV shows and movies.

Even when the days are long, Yara and Keri always take time to check in with each other. They make sure to rest and recharge so they have enough energy to make their dreams—and other artists' dreams—come true.

KERI, BORN AUGUST 19, 1969
YARA, BORN FEBRUARY 10, 2000
UNITED STATES OF AMERICA

ILLUSTRATION BY
NATALIA AGATTE

"MY MOM TAUGHT ME TO UNDERSTAND THAT I AM QUALIFIED FOR ANY OF THE CONVERSATIONS THAT I'M A PART OF, WHETHER IT'S WITH EXECUTIVES OR A SCHOOL PRINCIPAL. I'M SUPPOSED TO BE THERE."
—YARA SHAHIDI

KIM YESHI AND DECHEN YESHI

YAK WOOL CLOTHING MAKERS

High up in the mountains of Asia, there's a place called the Tibetan Plateau, where nomads live. Nomads are people who move around with their animals. These nomads raise yaks—big, hairy oxlike creatures that provide them with food and clothing. On the yaks' bellies grows a very soft fiber known as *khullu*, which keeps them warm during the long, snowy winters. Yaks shed their khullu every summer.

A woman named Kim, who was born in the United States but lived in India with her Tibetan husband, thought about the unused khullu. She loved Tibetan culture and knew nomads needed more jobs in their communities. Kim had an idea. *What if she worked with nomads to weave scarves from khullu?*

She asked her daughter, Dechen, to visit the nomads and see if they were interested. *No way*, said Dechen. But then she thought about it. She had just graduated from college and didn't have a job. So she went. At first, she was lonely. The nomads lived in tents, worked all day long, and were too busy to chat. Dechen started taking pictures and filming instead. Over time, she learned to love the people and the landscape, and they learned to trust her.

Few of the nomads had ever been to school. Families worked hard, but there were few job options, especially for women. By the time Kim joined her daughter on the plateau, many were excited to try something new. Kim and Dechen built a weaving workshop with plenty of natural light, heating, indoor plumbing, and a canteen. They even started a basketball team!

Khullu used to just float away in the wind. Now, it is used to provide stable jobs and make scarves, blankets, and clothes that sell all over the world.

KIM, BORN JANUARY 4, 1956
DECHEN, BORN MARCH 4, 1982
UNITED STATES OF AMERICA AND TIBET

"WE WANT TO MAKE SURE THAT PEOPLE WHO COLLECT FIBERS AND TURN THEM INTO LUXURY PRODUCTS ARE LOCAL TIBETANS AND THAT THE PROFIT WOULD GO SOLELY TO THE VILLAGERS."
—DECHEN YESHI

ILLUSTRATION BY
JING LI

LAURIE STRAND AND ARIANNA STRAND

PILOTS

Once upon a time, Arianna and her mother found themselves on a curious journey. They were flying through the sky in a tiny two-seater plane with a big brown pelican sitting in their luggage compartment.

Arianna's mom, Laurie, was a nurse who'd been flying for many years. As a child, Arianna loved to climb aboard and soar through the air with her mother holding firmly onto the controls. At 16, Arianna began flying on her own. And the day after she turned 17, Arianna got her pilot's license too.

One cold day in January, Laurie said to her daughter, "Find us somewhere fun to fly next week!" She'd been stressed at work and knew that going on an adventure with her daughter would soothe her nerves.

Little did Laurie know that Arianna had just read a very special message. A pelican needed help! It had been found nearly frozen in the Connecticut River. An animal rescue center in Florida was happy to nurse the pelican back to health. But how would the bird make the 1,200-mile trip to Florida?

"Mom, I have the perfect adventure for us!" Arianna said.

They named their feathered guest Arvy, after the RV-12 plane they'd take.

Arianna began plotting their course. They would stop for fuel only at places where a bird specialist could meet them. Laurie and Arianna switched off duties. One flew the plane while the other checked the weather or adjusted the GPS. All the while, Arvy made funny little grumbling noises in the background. Twelve hours later, the piloting pair (and their precious cargo) landed in Florida. It was the longest and most rewarding trip they'd taken together—and maybe the first of many rescue missions to come!

LAURIE, BORN APRIL 18, 1970
ARIANNA, BORN JULY 8, 2000
UNITED STATES OF AMERICA

"WHAT IS THE POINT OF SPENDING SO MUCH TIME AND MONEY FLYING IF YOU'RE NOT GOING TO HAVE FUN WHILE DOING IT?"
—ARIANNA STRAND

ILLUSTRATION BY JUI TALUKDER

LEENA SHARMA AND BHAKTI SHARMA

SCAN TO HEAR MORE!

SWIMMERS

Leena loved to swim, and she wanted her daughter to love it too. So one hot summer day, Leena took two-year-old Bhakti to a hotel and dropped her in the pool. Bhakti kicked and screamed, thrashing in the water. But soon, she was swimming with strong, smooth strokes. She could swim for hours on end, just like her mom.

By the time Bhakti was a teenager, she and Leena were swimming all over the world. They were even the first mother-daughter duo to swim across the English Channel! Bhakti was proud of her achievements, but there was something else she wanted to do—something so difficult only a few people had tried it before. Bhakti wanted to swim in the Southern Ocean.

As Bhakti's mother, Leena felt nervous. The water would be dangerously cold. But as Bhakti's coach, Leena knew she had to help her daughter achieve her dream.

Leena would fill a pool with ice. Then Bhakti would swim in the frigid water for 20 minutes before crawling out, her hands and feet numb. Leena would fill a blanket with hot water bags and help her daughter get warm again. This is how they trained for two years.

When Bhakti finally went to the Antarctic and plunged in, the water was so dense it felt like she was swimming in oil. She was about to give up when she saw a penguin swimming beside her. The penguin was cheering her on! She kept going. When she finally stepped out of the ocean, Bhakti's whole body was numb. But her heart was on fire. At the age of 25, she had broken the world record for the farthest swim—1.4 miles—in the Southern Ocean.

LEENA, BORN DECEMBER 7, 1965
BHAKTI, BORN NOVEMBER 30, 1989

INDIA

"AFTER EVERY SWIM, I HAVE DISCOVERED A NEW PART OF ME, MAYBE A NEW STRENGTH OR A NEW WEAKNESS."
—BHAKTI SHARMA

LINDA DAVIS AND SHARA DAVIS

HEALTH AIDES

Linda and her daughter Shara lived in an Alaskan island town that smelled like the sea. They loved walking along the sandy beaches in their big rubber boots. They also loved their community.

Mekoryuk was such a small fishing village that there were no doctors or hospitals. So Linda and Shara became health workers. They performed tests and check-ups and gave out medicine. They patched up scrapes, wrapped up sprains, and sent patients to the mainland for doctor visits or surgeries.

Linda and Shara worked through every challenge together. In 2020, they faced their biggest challenge yet: the Covid-19 virus.

When the pandemic began, people in Mekoryuk were worried. They didn't want to get sick or make anyone else sick. So they made sure to wear masks, check their temperatures, and keep their distance from others. No one on the island got sick because the villagers took the virus very seriously.

As soon as a vaccine was ready, Linda and Shara got it. Then they called each and every villager to encourage them to get vaccinated too. Some people were scared or confused, so Linda and Shara calmed their fears and answered all their questions. They went on the radio to reach all 200 members of their community.

The townspeople trusted Linda and Shara. And they wanted to get back to playing basketball and volleyball and listening to music together again. Thanks to the dedication of these two amazing health care workers, nearly 100 percent of the residents of Mekoryuk were quickly vaccinated. This devoted duo kept their community safe.

LINDA, BIRTHDATE UNKNOWN
SHARA, BIRTHDATE UNKNOWN
UNITED STATES OF AMERICA

"I LIKE WORKING WITH MY MOM. WE SUPPORT EACH OTHER A LOT, AND WE'RE ALWAYS THERE HELPING EACH OTHER."
—SHARA DAVIS

ILLUSTRATION BY XUAN LOC XUAN

LORAL QUINN AND EISHEL QUINN

ENTREPRENEURS

Once upon a time, a mother and a daughter covered their kitchen wall in sticky notes. Each one held an idea for a new business that would use technology to make a positive impact every day.

The idea they chose was all about using change to make change.

Every day, people buy things. They go to restaurants, toy stores, and pet shops, and order things online. Usually, the cost of a purchase doesn't add up to an even number, like $10. It's often more like $10.67. What happens to the extra 33 cents? Sometimes, stores ask if customers want to round up their change to give to charitable causes. *But what if we could collect change from* a lot *of people and use it to help the world?* thought Loral and Eishel.

They created an app that invited people to choose a charity, decide how much to give, and round up their extra change. One magical swipe of a credit or debit card and BOOM! Small amounts of change can be combined into big donations to schools, animal shelters, and organizations protecting the environment.

They named their app "Sustainably."

Other entrepreneurs started to notice Loral and Eishel's big idea. The pair won lots of awards, including a prize for being the start-up company of the year. Investors decided to provide funds for their business. Loral and Eishel were even able to quit their jobs to work on their app full time. Then they hired a whole team to help make their idea even bigger and better.

Every day, they add more charities to their list and invite more people to donate their change. They are helping the world one penny at a time.

LORAL, BIRTHDATE UNKNOWN
EISHEL, BORN 1995
UNITED KINGDOM

"HAVING MY AMAZING DAUGHTER, EISHEL, IS MY NUMBER ONE PERSONAL ACHIEVEMENT. BUT BEING NAMED BY RICHARD BRANSON AS HIS START-UP OF THE YEAR COMES PRETTY CLOSE."
—LORAL QUINN

ILLUSTRATION BY
KAREN GONZÁLEZ IBARRA

SCAN TO HEAR MORE!

MARIE CURIE AND IRÈNE JOLIOT-CURIE

SCIENTISTS

There once was a woman named Maria Sklodowska who believed that knowledge could heal the world.

Maria, also known as Marie, grew up in Poland in the late 1800s. She was the youngest of five children. Marie wasn't allowed to go to college because she was a girl. So she found a secret university where she studied hard—especially in science.

In 1895, Marie married a physics professor named Pierre Curie. Marie and Pierre were both fascinated by a new scientific discovery called radioactivity. Working in a lab, their hands swelled and their skin peeled as they tried to figure out how radioactivity worked. They discovered two new elements and were awarded Nobel Prizes for their incredible work.

The Curies had two daughters, Irène and Eve. Marie wanted her daughters to have the best education possible, so she taught them herself!

Young Irène joined her mom's research team, experimenting to find ways to use radiation to help heal people. During World War I, Marie developed small X-ray machines called "Les Petites Curies" (the Little Curies). She and Irène—who was just 17—braved the mud, danger, disease, and heartbreak of the front lines to help the wounded soldiers. They worked day and night, X-raying more than a million soldiers and helping to save countless lives. The pair also opened up a hospital for, and run entirely by, women.

During their incredible lives, they inspired each other and the world to push further and seek answers.

"Nothing in life is to be feared," said Marie. "It is only to be understood."

MARIE, NOVEMBER 7, 1867–JULY 4, 1934
IRÈNE, SEPTEMBER 12, 1897–MARCH 17, 1956
POLAND AND FRANCE

ILLUSTRATION BY
KASIA BOGDAŃSKA

"LIFE IS NOT EASY FOR ANY OF US.
BUT WHAT OF THAT? WE MUST HAVE
PERSEVERANCE AND, ABOVE ALL,
CONFIDENCE IN OURSELVES."
—MARIE CURIE

NAJATE LEKLYE AND MERYEM SLIMANI

FASHION INFLUENCERS

When Meryem was a baby, she moved from Morocco to the Netherlands with her mother, Najate. But Najate just couldn't imagine having strangers look after her little girl while she went to work as a teacher. So she sent baby Meryem back to Morocco to live with her parents. There, Meryem went everywhere her grandfather went and loved to daydream, looking up at the sky.

At four years old, Meryem returned to the Netherlands. But she felt like an outsider. She barely remembered her mother, and no one at school understood her when she spoke Arabic. Eventually, she learned to speak Dutch, but she was depressed. She didn't feel like she belonged.

Meryem started a style blog where she could exercise her creativity. She asked Najate to photograph her so they could spend time together. Their bond grew stronger. But the blog didn't take off.

Frustrated, Meryem thought about giving up. But then, she had a wild idea. *What if I made my mom the model?* she thought.

She gave it a shot. And it worked! People on social media could not get enough of 67-year-old Najate fearlessly sporting a tiger-print hijab with an oversized neon blazer. They loved her cheetah-print dresses and the way she paired sneakers and a suit with mirrored sunglasses.

Each picture Meryem and her mom created challenged the notion that people have to look a certain way to belong. Today, these former outsiders stand together at the center of a cultural shift where they—and many others—celebrate women of every shape, age, color, and culture.

NAJATE, BORN OCTOBER 29, 1952
MERYEM, BORN JULY 29, 1983
MOROCCO AND THE NETHERLANDS

"IT'S OKAY TO BE YOU, IT'S OKAY TO BE DIFFERENT, IT'S OKAY TO CHOOSE YOUR OWN PATH."
—MERYEM SLIMANI

ILLUSTRATION BY
ANASTASIA MAGLOIRE WILLIAMS

NIVEDITHA SHETTY HEGDE AND ISHANVI HEGDE

DANCERS

Once there was a girl named Niveditha—Nivi for short—who was mesmerized by her mother's dance moves. She watched as her mom swept her arms out in rippling waves. She marveled as her mom kicked one leg high while balancing on the other.

And her mom wasn't even a trained dancer!

Nivi wanted to move and spin and swirl just like her mom. So her mother taught her everything she knew. Nivi had no idea that 30 years later, she'd be teaching her daughter Ishanvi how to dance too.

When Ishanvi's nursery school teachers showed Nivi a video of the four-year-old bopping and prancing, Nivi knew her little girl had the dancing gene. She started showing Ishanvi how to do classical Indian dances. They had so much fun they started making up their own steps.

Nivi and Ishanvi treated each number like a professional performance. Sometimes they would dress up in matching saris, with a maang tikka glittering on their foreheads and beaded bangles on their wrists, and perform at home. Other times, they would throw on the same tank top and shorts (in their own sizes, of course!) and perform at the beach, the ocean waves dancing behind them.

Ishanvi's dad thought their routines were so cool he started filming them. Nivi posted a video online. A friend shared the clip, then another reposted it, and then another, until they had more than 1.5 million subscribers!

Sharing their videos with the world is fun. But Nivi and Ishanvi's favorite thing about creating new dances is sharing what they love with each other.

NIVEDITHA, BORN JUNE 12, 1984
ISHANVI, BORN APRIL 3, 2014
INDIA AND UNITED ARAB EMIRATES

ILLUSTRATION BY
CHAAYA PRABHAT

"THE LOVE AND HARD WORK YOU PUT INTO DOING SOMETHING ALWAYS SHOWS, AND THAT'S WHAT MAKES IT FRUITFUL."
—NIVEDITHA SHETTY HEGDE

PORTIA MBAU AND LUMAI DE SMIDT

CHEF AND PHOTOGRAPHER

SCAN TO HEAR MORE!

Once there was a chef named Portia who stood over a burbling pot of Cameroonian groundnut stew. She stirred, sniffed, and made sure to add just the right combination of garlic, ginger, and cayenne pepper.

As a young woman, Portia looked around and saw that there were no African restaurants in Johannesburg, where she lived. She began to travel all around South Africa, sampling foods. Then she went to college in the United States. Her new friends from Ethiopia, Cameroon, Nigeria, Mali, and other countries introduced her to their favorite dishes.

When Portia returned to South Africa, she opened a restaurant in Cape Town. She wanted to make sure people could sample flavors from all over the continent. The Africa Cafe quickly became popular with locals and visitors from all over the world. Everyone loved Portia's cooking!

"I must have your recipe," customers said. "What's the secret ingredient?"

"The secret to tasty food comes in layering spices and herbs. That's the alchemy I love," Portia replied with a twinkle in her eye.

One day, her daughter Lumai said, "Why don't we publish a cookbook?"

Portia wrote down her delicious, healthy recipes. She made sure to put in customer favorites like Moroccan herb salad, cassava bread, Malawi mbatata, Soweto chakalaka, Malagasy calamari, and Nigerian suya. Lumai took photos of the food and designed the book. She made each morsel look so delectable that readers wanted to eat Portia's food right off the page.

In 2020, they launched their own brand of sauces, dips, teas, spice mixes, and more. This delightful duo hopes to send African flavors all over the world.

PORTIA, BORN JUNE 27, 1960
LUMAI, BORN NOVEMBER 16, 1992

SOUTH AFRICA

"WHEN I WAS GROWING UP, THE KITCHEN WAS MY PLAYGROUND."
— PORTIA MBAU

ILLUSTRATION BY
FANESHA FABRE

PRUE LEITH AND LI-DA KRUGER

TV HOST AND FILMMAKER

Once upon a time, a baby was born in Cambodia. Sadly, the country was at war. At just six months old, Li-Da was left at an orphanage and later flown out of the country.

Prue first met Li-Da in Paris. She smiled as she looked at the baby's chubby cheeks and listened to her coos and squeaks. Right away, Prue knew in her heart that she was going to be Li-Da's mother.

Back home in England, people stared at Li-Da and wanted to know why her skin was so much darker than Prue's. Sometimes, they said mean things or refused to believe Prue was her mother.

A chef, Prue opened restaurants, wrote cookbooks, and became a well-known TV personality. Li-Da grew up and became a filmmaker. She decided she wanted to find her birth family so she could show her own adopted son where they came from. Prue tried not to worry that Li-Da would disappear from her life if she found her Cambodian relatives. "I support you 100 percent trying to find your birth parents," she told her daughter.

Li-Da and Prue traveled across Cambodia. They visited tiny villages and bustling cities and tried traditional foods. Prue choked up as she saw tiny children who looked like Li-Da as a baby, running around with chubby cheeks and smiling faces. They met many, many people on their search for Li-Da's birth family. They even filmed a documentary about the journey.

Li-Da didn't find her birth parents on that trip. But she learned a lot about her culture and heritage. Every day, she's learning more and more about her homeland with her proud mum Prue at her side.

PRUE, BORN FEBRUARY 18, 1940
LI-DA, BORN CIRCA 1975
UNITED KINGDOM AND CAMBODIA

ILLUSTRATION BY
DANIELLE ELYSSE MANN

"IT'S NOT BECAUSE I WANT ANOTHER PARENT, I HAVE PRUE. BUT AS A CHILD WHO ESCAPED THE CAMBODIAN GENOCIDE, I AM DESPERATE TO FIND MY BIOLOGICAL FAMILY AND MAKE SENSE OF MY PAST."
—LI-DA KRUGER

SARAH KETTLE AND SALLY KETTLE

ROWERS

Once upon a time, there was a girl named Sally who found herself in the middle of the Atlantic Ocean in a tiny rowboat with her mom, Sarah. They were about 1,500 miles from any land and headed in the wrong direction!

"Oh, I hope the wind changes," Sally moaned. "I hope the weather changes."

"Stop!" said Sarah. "Hope doesn't help!" Sally knew her mom was right. Just hoping for the winds or weather to change wouldn't get them anywhere. They had to track the currents, plot their course, and row!

Growing up, Sally wanted to try everything—from running marathons to launching into space. When she was 26, she trained for a 3,000-mile rowing race with her boyfriend. But a few days into their journey, he got sick, and they had to turn back. That's when Sally called her mom.

Sally and Sarah didn't always get along. While Sally loved to travel and sing out loud, Sarah loved gardening and being quiet at home. They fought a lot. But now that Sally was an adult, she felt like she and her mom shared something important—a sense of adventure.

In January 2004, Sally and Sarah pushed off from the Canary Islands. Every hour, they switched who was rowing. They tried to switch at night, but it was too hard to row alone in the dark. So they both slept and let the boat drift. There were days when it was brutally cold and lonely. There were also times when they laughed about their weird dreams or how much they missed walking their dogs. But after 106 days, Sally and Sarah made it to the other side of the Atlantic. Together, they could do anything!

SARAH, BORN DECEMBER 8, 1958
SALLY, BORN MARCH 8, 1977
UNITED KINGDOM

"IT'S SOMETIMES NOT WHAT YOU DO, BUT WHAT YOU INSPIRE OTHERS TO DO THAT REALLY MAKES A DIFFERENCE."
—SALLY KETTLE

SHAUNA MULLINS AND GEORGIA ROSS

PHOTOGRAPHER AND MODEL

Once upon a time, there was a girl who loved to dress up. But she didn't dress up like princesses or superheroes. She dressed up like real-life Black women from history.

At seven, Georgia was a curious kid. Her mom, Shauna, was a stellar teacher who taught her kids at home. Their loving family was built through adoption, and the pair embarked on a project to explore Georgia's cultural roots. They would read about amazing Black scientists, singers, athletes, and surgeons. Each time Georgia discovered someone she liked, she would dress up and become that person. Then Shauna would snap a picture.

Georgia put on a lab coat and suddenly became Dr. Marie Maynard Daly, the first Black woman to earn a PhD in chemistry. Georgia imagined herself mixing together liquids in test tubes and beakers. With the right tools, maybe she could whip up a cure for a disease or invent an important chemical compound.

Then, she shrugged out of her lab coat and into an old-fashioned dress and thick-rimmed glasses. With a guitar balanced on her lap, she closed her eyes. She'd become Elizabeth Cotten, a legendary folk singer and musician.

Shauna wrote a story to go with every woman featured in their photo shoots. She and Georgia wanted to share their project with curious girls everywhere. So they started a website called She Made History.

Each time they dress up, take a photo, write a new story, or get a friendly comment from a fan, they feel proud—proud of their own creativity and proud to share exciting stories of strong Black women from throughout history.

SHAUNA, BORN AUGUST 6, 1970
GEORGIA, BORN JUNE 11, 2009
UNITED STATES OF AMERICA

"IMAGINE IF EVERY LITTLE GIRL GREW UP LEARNING ABOUT THESE EXTRAORDINARY WOMEN. THEY WOULD NEVER DOUBT THEIR PLACE IN THE WORLD OR THEIR OWN LIMITLESS POSSIBILITIES."
—SHAUNA MULLINS

ILLUSTRATION BY MONICA MIKAI

SUSAN HOLLAND AND BRITTNEY WACASEY

BARREL RACERS

Once there was a girl named Brittney who rode a horse at lightning speed. She was headed straight toward a barrel. But Brittney wasn't scared. In fact, she felt courageous and calm.

"Ready . . . Here!" called her mom, Susan, through a walkie-talkie. Brittney turned the horse just in time to race around the barrel, her blond ponytail flapping in the wind behind her.

"Since I'm legally blind, I can't see the barrels until I'm going around them," Brittney says. "So I have to listen to Mom." And her mom sure knows what she's talking about. Susan competed in barrel racing for 20 years.

After Brittney was born, doctors explained that her eyes were underdeveloped and that she'd never see. The family visited many different doctors and tried many different therapies. Brittney gained a little bit of sight in her left eye. She says it's like looking through a tiny straw at blurry images. But she cannot see out of her right eye at all.

When she was four, Brittney begged her mom to teach her how to ride barrels. Up there in the saddle, Brittney felt fearless and free. She couldn't wait to go faster and start racing like her mom. So, a few years later, the two of them came up with the walkie-talkie idea. Susan would sit in the stands and give precise instructions while Brittney listened on a headset and galloped and guided her horse around the barrels.

Of course, there have been stumbles and falls. But Brittney always got back on her horse. She sensed the horse's strength, trusted her own inner vision, and smiled at the crowd as her mother's cheers filled her ears.

SUSAN, BORN DECEMBER 13 (YEAR UNKNOWN)
BRITTNEY, BIRTHDATE UNKNOWN
UNITED STATES

"I JUST WANT TO TRY TO GET AS GOOD AS I CAN. A FAST TIME OR SLOW TIME DOESN'T MATTER. JUST RIDING HORSES IS FUN."
—BRITTNEY WACASEY

ILLUSTRATION BY EMMA PEDERSEN

TANIA HALIK AND MARTINA HALIK

CROSS-COUNTRY SKIERS

Once upon a time, a girl named Martina and her mother, Tania, set out on an epic journey. Together, they would cross-country ski the length of Canada's Coast Mountains.

Tania dehydrated food like fruit, nuts, meat, and granola in her kitchen. The packages of food filled up the living room. They couldn't possibly carry it all! They had to have it flown by helicopter to special food drop sites. Still, they would need to carry a two-person tent, sleeping bags, a change of warm clothes, an emergency kit, a camp cook stove, glacier-climbing gear, and a blow-up raft so they could get across any rivers in their path.

After a year of planning, Martina and Tania set off from Squamish, British Columbia. Each day, they walked, skied, and climbed a sea of ice, rock, and snow. Each night, they made camp to try to warm up.

The wind whipped around their little orange tent. It shuddered and shivered as if trying to shake off snow flurries. Martina and Tania savored their hot chocolate and cuddled up in their sleeping bags for warmth.

The trip was grueling. But it was also filled with unforgettable beauty. Glittering fields stretched as far as the eye could see. Mountaintops jutted out of fluffy pillows of snow. They gazed in awe at a piercing blue ice cave that rose up around them like a frozen cathedral.

Finally, six months after their journey began, Martina and Tania emerged from the forest. They arrived in Skagway, Alaska, on a rainy, cold day in early spring. With huge grins, they hugged each other and cried.

Tania and Martina were the first team of women to make this journey.

TANIA, BIRTHDATE UNKNOWN
MARTINA, BIRTHDATE UNKNOWN

CANADA

ILLUSTRATION BY
ANJA REPONEN

"WE KNOW ONE ANOTHER
REALLY WELL. WE KNOW
WHEN TO TAKE CARE OF
ONE ANOTHER."
—MARTINA HALIK

VALENTINA QUINTERO AND ARIANNA ARTEAGA QUINTERO

TRAVEL GUIDES

Once there was a girl named Arianna whose mother, Valentina, traveled all the time. Valentina was a TV and radio personality who encouraged Venezuelans to explore their country. She even wrote guidebooks to help make traveling easier. Valentina secretly wished that one day her daughter would join her on her adventures.

But Arianna didn't want to write guidebooks. She wanted to be a dancer or make movies—anything but travel all the time. She didn't want to spend time on cramped buses and rickety little planes.

But then she grew up. One day, she found her mother upset and stressed out. *I have so much to do and so little time!* Valentina cried. Arianna rolled up her sleeves and said, *Okay, I'll help.*

Arianna was organized and full of ideas. And soon Valentina's secret dream came true: she and her daughter became cohosts of a show called *Two on a Trip*. They would travel all over their beloved country.

Venezuela is filled with beauty. It has waterfalls, jungles, mountains, beaches, and charming towns. But it has problems too. Many citizens don't have electricity or enough food to eat. The duo recognize the country's hardships, while also showing off its beauty, culture, and community.

Traveling together can be tough though. *Mom snores*, says Arianna. *My daughter is impatient*, says Valentina. But they make each other laugh all the time. They trust each other and know they can always be honest.

For Valentina and Arianna, every day is an adventure that they share with each other and the world.

VALENTINA, BORN JUNE 28, 1954
ARIANNA, BORN NOVEMBER 25, 1980
VENEZUELA

ILLUSTRATION BY
CARIBAY MB

"IF I HAVE THE ABILITY
TO SEE THE BEAUTIFUL
IN THE MIDST OF THE
MISFORTUNE AND THE ASHES,
IT IS MY RESPONSIBILITY
TO SHOW IT TO OTHERS."
—ARIANNA ARTEAGA QUINTERO

WRITE YOUR STORY

DRAW YOUR PORTRAIT

MORE FUN TOGETHER!

These activities were designed by author Eve Rodsky for you to do with your mom or other beloved grown-up. Have fun!

BE THE TEACHER

Sally Kettle had an unforgettable time sharing her love of rowing with her mom. Niveditha Shetty Hegde loved teaching traditional Indian dances to her daughter. What is something you'd like to share with your grown-up or your child? Find pens and some paper and do the activity below.

1. Do you love to paint pictures, bake cookies, or build birdhouses? What can you do for hours on end and never get bored? Make a list of three creative things you love to do.
2. Share your lists with each other. Explain what you love most about the activities on your list.
3. Select one activity from each other's list and then teach one another, step by step, how to do it. Remember to be patient!

SHOW AND TELL!

Briana Sullivan played her guitar every night before bed while she and her daughter were hiking the Appalachian Trail. They will both always love that instrument! We all have things we hold on to because they remind us of an important person or time in our lives. These objects are special because of the feelings they give us. Do you have an object or a keepsake that makes you happy?

1. Find an object from around your home that is meaningful to you—something that makes you happy or reminds you of a specific memory.
2. Present your objects to one another. Explain where and when you got them, what they mean to you, and why they are special.

SAY IT LOUD, SAY IT PROUD

Beyoncé's heart swelled when her daughter said she was proud of her. But you don't have to be famous or rich to make a big impact on the people around you. It feels really good to be proud of a loved one. And it's important to share your feelings. What does your grown-up or child do that makes you feel proud?

1. Think of all the cool things about your grown-up or child. Make a list of three things that make you proud of her.
2. Write a letter explaining what those three things are and why they are important to you.
3. Share your letters with each other. You can hand them over or read them aloud—whatever you choose!

THE STORY OF YOUR LIFE

When Arianna Arteaga Quintero and her mom traveled around Venezuela filming their TV show, they had lots of time to share the stories of their lives. Take some time to share memories with each other. This activity is even more fun with snacks! So pop some popcorn or cut up some fruit and get ready for a trip down memory lane.

1. Think of your favorite memories of something you two did together. Try to remember all of the details.
2. You know the story best from your point of view. Now, try to imagine the same memory from the point of view of your grown-up or child.
3. Grab a pen and paper and write the story from the other person's point of view. Feel free to add pictures too!
4. Swap stories so you can each read what the other came up with.
5. Tell each other what you like most about each story.

WHAT MATTERS MOST TO YOU?

Julie Andrews and Emma Walton Hamilton pour their joy and creativity into the books they write together. You can learn a lot about yourself and your friends and family by talking about the values that are most important to you.

1. Take a look at the list of values below.

adventurousness	fun	mindfulness
courage	hard work	power
creativity	honesty	respect
curiosity	humor	self-expression
dependability	joy	sharing
fairness	kindness	teamwork
forgiveness	leadership	thoughtfulness
friendship	love	trustworthiness

2. Pick three values that are most important to you.
3. Share your top three values with each other and talk about what these values mean to you.
4. Write your names and your three values on a sheet of paper. Decorate with drawings and patterns. Hang up your colorful poster if you'd like!

A TRADITION FOR TWO

Martina and Tania Halik spent six months on an epic cross-country ski trip. Martina said, "We know when to take care of one another." Everyone feels sad or mad sometimes. One way to support the people you love is to set up a ritual to help you when you're feeling down.

1. Make up something that is just for the two of you. This could be a secret handshake, a silly dance, or a short poem that you both can memorize and say to one another when you need a boost.
2. Write down the details of your special ritual on two sheets of paper. That way, you can each have a copy. Put it somewhere special in case you ever need to remind yourself about your bonding ritual.

DISCOVER YOUR UNICORN SPACE

"Unicorn Space" is the space you get when you have the free time to do something that brings you joy and makes you a better you. It is time when you can explore your curiosity without being rushed or interrupted. Set aside some time when you both can answer the questions below and spend time doing something you love.

1. Write, draw, or act out your answers to the questions below.

   What are you curious about?

   What's something you do that is so much fun you lose track of time?

   What is a hobby, skill, or idea you'd like to learn more about soon?

2. Fill in the blanks in these sentences.

   I would like more time to explore _____.

   I have always wanted to learn about _____.

   I have always wanted to make a _____.

3. Take some time to do an activity on your list. If it is hard to find the time to dedicate to enjoying your Unicorn Space, work together to set aside some stress-free time to play!

ABOUT EVE RODSKY

Eve Rodsky and her mom have always been a powerful pair! Growing up with a single mom in New York City, Eve saw firsthand how much hard work her mom had to do every day. When Eve went to college, she studied economics and anthropology and then got a law degree. She worked high-powered jobs advising people how to give money generously and support those in need. After working with hundreds of families, Eve realized that what she loved most was helping people find balance and peace in their homes. She wrote a book called *Fair Play: A Game-Changing Solution for When You Have Too Much to Do (and More Life to Live),* and it became a *New York Times* best seller! Her newest book, *Find Your Unicorn Space,* is an inspirational guide to setting personal goals and unleashing your creativity. Eve lives in Los Angeles with her husband and their three children.

MORE STORIES!

For more stories about amazing women and girls, check out other Rebel Girls books.

LISTEN TO MORE EMPOWERING STORIES ON THE REBEL GIRLS APP!

Download the app to listen to beloved Rebel Girls stories, as well as brand-new tales of extraordinary women. Filled with the adventures and accomplishments of women from around the world and throughout history, the Rebel Girls app is designed to entertain, inspire, and build confidence in listeners everywhere.

THE ILLUSTRATORS

Twenty-three extraordinary female artists from all over the world illustrated the portraits in this book. Here are their names.

ANASTASIA MAGLOIRE WILLIAMS, USA, 39

ANDRESSA MEISSNER, BRAZIL, 23

ANJA REPONEN, FINLAND, 53

BÁRBARA TAMILIN, BRAZIL, 17

CARIBAY MB, ARGENTINA, 55

CHAAYA PRABHAT, INDIA, 41

DANIELLE ELYSSE MANN, USA, 45

DEANDRA HODGE, USA, 9

DEBBY RAHMALIA, INDONESIA, 31

EMMA PEDERSEN, CANADA, 51

FANESHA FABRE, USA, 21, 43

JENNIFER M. POTTER, USA, 19

JING LI, CHINA, 27

JUI TALUKDER, USA, 29

KAREN GONZÁLEZ IBARRA, MEXICO, 35

KASIA BOGDAŃSKA, POLAND, 37

LAYLIE FRAZIER, USA, 7, 15

MONICA MIKAI, USA, 49

NAN CAO, USA, 11

NATALIA AGATTE, BRAZIL, 25

SONIA PULIDO, SPAIN, 47

TATSIANA BURGAUD, FRANCE, 13

XUAN LOC XUAN, VIETNAM, 33

ABOUT REBEL GIRLS

REBEL GIRLS is a global, multi-platform empowerment brand dedicated to helping raise the most inspired and confident global generation of girls through content, experiences, products, and community. Originating from an international best-selling children's book, Rebel Girls amplifies stories of real-life, extraordinary women throughout history, geography, and field of excellence. With a growing community of nearly 20 million self-identified Rebel Girls spanning more than 100 countries, the brand engages with Generation Alpha through its book series, award-winning podcast, events, and merchandise.

Join the Rebel Girls community:

- Facebook: facebook.com/rebelgirls
- Instagram: @rebelgirls
- Twitter: @rebelgirlsbook
- Web: rebelgirls.com
- Podcast: rebelgirls.com/podcast

If you liked this book, please take a moment to review it wherever you prefer!